will.i.am

Music and Style Sensation

This paperback edition published in 2016
First published in 2014 by Wayland
Copyright © Wayland 2014

Wayland, an imprint of
Hachette Children's Group
Part of Hodder & Stoughton
Carmelite House
50 Victoria Embankment
London EC4Y 0DZ

Senior editor: Julia Adams

Produced for Wayland by Dynamo
Written by Hettie Bingham

PICTURE ACKNOWLEDGEMENTS:
Key: b=bottom, t=top, r= right, l=left, m=middle,
bgd=background

Getty Images: p1 m, p2 tr, p4 m, p5 tr, p5 bl, p10 m, p11 r, p13 m, p15 br, p15 ml, 18 bl, p21 m, p24 mr, p27 t, p29 br, p30 ml Getty Images; p8 br. **Shutterstock:** Backgrounds and Doodles: VikaSuh, tsaplia, nmfotograf, Aleks Melnik, Liashko, armo.rs, topform, MisterElements, PinkPueblo, snapgalleria, Slanapotam, kstudija, Marie Nimrichterova, Cidonia, blue67design, MisterElements, p1 m Christian Bertrand, p6 m Vacclav, p6b and 7b Ray_of_Light, p16 l Christian Bertrand, p21 l Ann Precious, p22b and 23b Ray_of_Light, p23 ml spirit of america, p25 Alexey Belonogov, p26 bl Alex_Po. **Splash News:** P14 mr YFrog; p17 bl Rick Davis.

Dewey classification: 782.4'21649'092-dc23

ISBN 978 0 7502 8947 4
Library e-book ISBN 978 0 7502 8777 7
Printed in China
10 9 8 7 6 5 4 3 2 1

An Hachette UK company
www.hachette.co.uk
www.hachettechildrens.co.uk

CONTENTS

will.i.am

will.i.am
Music and Style Sensation

'MUSIC IS LIKE AIR TO ME; I HAVE TO DO IT TO SURVIVE... IT FILLS UP MY LUNGS WITH LOVELINESS.'

■ Singer-songwriter, producer, performer, DJ, philanthropist and entrepreneur – will.i.am is a man of many talents. From life in the LA projects (USA) to hanging out with the President of the United States of America, his fame and fortune is a richly deserved reward for his hard work and determination.

NAME: William James Adams

BORN: 15 March 1975

MOTHER: Debra Cain

HOMETOWN: Los Angeles, USA

SCHOOLS: Palisades Middle School and Palisades High School, LA, USA

OCCUPATION: Singer–songwriter, composer, record producer, voice actor, businessman, dancer, DJ, rapper, philanthropist

FAMOUS FOR: The Black Eyed Peas, The Voice and working with countless mega stars

That's Cool!

When he first saw his birth certificate at the age of 25, will.i.am learned that he had been named after the father he had never met, William Adams. His mother told him: 'That's not your dad – I'm your dad. That's a very powerful name that you have. You've utilized it. It's his fault that he didn't live up to that name.'

In the
Projects

Los Angeles is a city that many people associate with movie stars and glamorous lifestyles, but like most places, LA has areas of social housing which are very different from the Hollywood mansions of the stars.

Born in East Los Angeles, will.i.am grew up in the Estrada Courts housing projects in Boyle Heights. Housing projects are government-owned housing schemes for people on low incomes. Estrada Courts is owned by the city of Los Angeles and was built in 1942. It is known for the many colourful murals that are found on the estate.

Boyle Heights is a mainly Hispanic area and this was reflected in the culture that influenced will.i.am's early life. 'Every Sunday we'd eat at El Tepeyak on Evergreen [Avenue],' he said, talking of his life in the projects. This is a popular Mexican restaurant which has been run by the same family for four generations.

As a kid, will.i.am was inspired by the music of Michael Jackson. 'I used to try and dance like him,' he once said. Later will.i.am was to work for Jackson, something he could only dream of as a child (see page 14).

Will.i.am attended kindergarten at Lorena Street Elementary School in Boyle Heights, but from fifth grade he travelled to a middle school in Pacific Palisades. During the holidays he went to the summer school at Stevenson Middle School, which was closer to where he lived.

That's Cool!

When will.i.am became rich, he moved his extended family out of the projects to another area in Los Angeles called Sherman Oaks. His grandma and aunt were the last of his family to leave the projects in 2010.
(see page 24).

'THE PROJECTS TO ME WAS WONDERFUL BECAUSE OF THE JOY FOR LIFE; THAT'S ALL YOU HAVE IS LIFE. THAT'S ALL YOU HAVE IS FRIENDS AND FAMILY. I'M LIVING PROOF OF WHATEVER YOU'RE BORN INTO, YOUR TOMORROW COULD BE TOTALLY DIFFERENT.'

'I'M NOT IN EAST LOS ANGELES ANYMORE, BUT I MISS IT. I NEVER HAD TACOS BETTER THAN THEY GOT THERE.'

When will.i.am was young he played American football for the East LA Bobcats. He has fond memories of this time and has spoken of 'Coach Andy' and the team he used to practise with at Salazar Park, near where he lived. He also played basketball at nearby Costello Park, a place where his mother still works with children in after-school programmes.

'TO KNOW WHERE YOU'RE GOING, YOU GOT TO KNOW WHERE YOU CAME FROM.'

The Music Begins

From his early childhood, will.i.am had music in his life. His mother used to listen to 1970s disco grou[p] Earth, Wind and Fire while she was doing the housework a[nd] will.i.am was a big fan of Michael Jackson. As he grew olde[r] he dreamed of being part of the music scene.

When will.i.am was 10, his mother wanted something better for her son than what was on offer in Boyle Heights, so she sent him to school in Pacific Palisades, West Los Angeles. She wanted him to be challenged and arranged for him to sit a scholarship exam, which he passed, securing him a place at Palisades Middle School.

Will.i.am's mother always encouraged him to be an individual. He did that by wearing bright clothes to stand out.

'I TOOK SAFETY IN DRESSING UP SO PEOPLE KNEW ME TO BE DIFFERENT.'

'EVER SINCE I WAS TWELVE, I WANTED TO MOVE MY MOM OUT OF THE NEIGHBOURHOOD. SO THAT WAS MY DREAM. YOU DON'T HAVE A DREAM FOR NOTHING, USUALLY DREAMS COME FROM SOMETHING.'

Will.i.am didn't think of himself as being 'poor' until a charity campaign at his school made him realise he was from a poor family.

Will.i.am once explained:

'I was in fifth grade and we had to bring canned foods into school and at the time I didn't know who the 'poor people' were.

I came back home and was like,

"Mom, I need to bring canned foods to school."

And she was like,

"Boy, you ain't taking no canned foods to school."'

It was only when he later saw pupils from his school delivering the donated cans in his own neighbourhood that he realized he was one of the 'poor people'.

Atban Klann was renamed Black Eyed Pods and then later became The Black Eyed Peas.

'I had the dream of being a hip-hop artist, and when I was in the 11th grade, I got my first record deal. I formed the Black Eyed Peas in 1995.'

will.i.am, 2013

When will.i.am moved up to Palisades Charter High School, he met Allan Pineda Lindo, who renamed himself as apl.de.ap (pronounced apple de app). At that time will.i.am was known as Will 1X. Along with their friends Mookie Mook, DJ Motiv8 (Monroe Walker) and Dante Santiago, they formed the hip hop group, Atban Klan. The group was signed to Ruthless Records in 1992 and made their debut on an EP by Eazy-E. Atban Klann stayed with Ruthless Records until they were dropped from the label after Eazy-E died in 1995.

The Black Eyed Peas

More than just a hip hop group, the Black Eyed Peas take influences from R&B, pop and dance music. They have sold more than 50 million records worldwide.

The Black Eyed Peas as we know the group today emerged from former work by will.i.am and apl.de.ap. They had begun rapping and performing around Los Angeles when they were in eighth grade together, back in 1988.

That's Cool!

Before Fergie joined the group, the Black Eyed Peas had approached singer Nicole Scherzinger. She had to turn them down as she was contracted to the band Eden's Crush at the time. She went on to be the lead singer of the Pussycat Dolls before pursuing a solo career.

In 1995, Taboo joined will.i.am and apl.de.ap and the Black Eyed Peas were formed. Although the group achieved cult status, their popularity was slow to build. Things began to change in 2002 when Fergie joined the band and they developed a more 'poppy' sound. By 2003, all their hard work paid off when they had their first major hit with the single *Where is the Love?* from their third album, *Elephunk*.

First album: *Behind the Front*, 1998
A single from this album was used in the soundtrack for the movie *Bulworth*, released the same year.

Second album: *Bridging the Gap*, 2000 The singles *Weekends*, featuring Esthero, and *Request Line*, featuring R&B singer, Macy Gray, were released.

Third album: *Elephunk*, 2003
This was the first album that featured Fergie's vocals. The single *Where is the Love?* was released and topped the charts in thirteen countries.

Fourth album: *Monkey Business*, 2005
The singles released from this album were *Don't Phunk with My Heart*, *Don't Lie*, *My Humps* and *Pump it*. They were all big hits.

Fifth album: *The E.N.D* (The energy never dies), 2009 This album evolved a new 'electro hop' style. The singles *Boom Boom Pow*, *I Gotta Feeling*, *Meet Me Half Way*, *Imma Be* and *Rock That Body* were all massive hits.

Sixth album: *The Beginning*, 2010
The Time, *Just Can't Get Enough* and *Don't Stop the Party* were released as singles from this album. It is their last album released to date, although will.i.am has mentioned a possible seventh album, so watch this space!

The Group Members
Front man **will.i.am** is joined by:

Allan Pineda Lindo a.k.a apl.de.ap Born in the Philippines, he came to live in the United States when he was a teenager. He studied with will.i.am at Palisades High School.

Jaime Gómez a.k.a Taboo Like will.i.am, he grew up in Boyle Heights.

Stacy Ann Ferguson a.k.a Fergie She grew up in one of LA's more affluent neighbourhoods. She studied dance and was a voiceover artist for cartoons when she was a kid. She was also a straight A student and a cheerleader at school.

will.i.am Solo

While he was recording and touring with the Black Eyed Peas and working with a host of other stars, he was also busy with his own material; he released four studio albums between 2001 and 2013.

2001

LOST CHANGE WAS RELEASED IN 2001 ON THE BBE (BARELY BREAKING EVEN) RECORD LABEL. IT WAS RELEASED AS PART OF THE LABEL'S 'BEAT GENERATION' SERIES. NO SINGLES WERE RELEASED FROM THIS ALBUM, ALTHOUGH THERE WAS A MUSIC VIDEO MADE FOR THE TRACK 'I AM'.

2003

WILL.I.AM'S SECOND SOLO ALBUM, MUST BE 21, WAS RELEASED IN 2003. THE TRACK GO! WAS OFTEN USED AS THE THEME FOR LIVE BASKETBALL AND NATIONAL FOOTBALL LEAGUE GAMES IN 2005. A VIDEO FOR THIS TRACK WAS ALSO MADE FOR USE WITHIN THESE SPORTS, BUT ONCE AGAIN NO SINGLES WERE RELEASED FROM THE ALBUM.

2007

THE THIRD ALBUM, SONGS ABOUT GIRLS, WAS RELEASED IN 2007. THE TRACK I GOT IT FROM MY MAMA WAS RELEASED AND MADE IT TO NO.31 IN THE AMERICAN CHARTS. TWO MORE SINGLES WERE RELEASED FROM THIS ALBUM – HEARTBREAKER AND ONE MORE CHANCE.

2013

#WILLPOWER, WILL.I.AM'S FOURTH ALBUM, WAS RELEASED IN 2013. IT WAS ORIGINALLY SCHEDULED FOR RELEASE IN 2011 UNDER THE TITLE BLACK EINSTEIN. THE FIRST SINGLE RELEASE FROM THIS ALBUM, *THIS IS LOVE*, FEATURED THE VOCALS OF EVA SIMONS AND REACHED NO.1 IN THE UK CHARTS. *SCREAM AND SHOUT* WAS THE SECOND SINGLE RELEASED. THIS FEATURED BRITNEY SPEARS. JUSTIN BIEBER APPEARS ON THE THIRD SINGLE FROM THIS ALBUM, #THATPOWER.

That's Cool!

In August 2012, will.i.am became the first recording star to send a song to Mars. He did this in conjunction with NASA's Curiosity Mars Space Lab; Reach for the Stars (Mars Edition) was played back from Mars during a youth education event hosted by NASA's Jet Propulsion Laboratory.

will.i.am
Collaborates

From Michael Jackson to Britney Spears, there are few mega stars that do not feature on the long list of will.i.am's collaborations.

will.i.am with Britney Spears in the recording studio

When Michael Jackson was looking for a fresh sound in 2006, he turned to will.i.am for some ideas. When asked why he wanted to work with will.i.am, Michael Jackson said: 'Because I think he's doing wonderful, innovative, positive, great music.' will.i.am responded by saying: 'This is like a dream come true for me, you know.'

When will.i.am worked with Britney Spears in 2013, they became close friends. He was collaborating with Britney on her eighth studio album, Britney Jean. Before a single note was recorded, will.i.am and Britney spent weeks getting to know each other. will.i.am wanted to know what made her happy, things she liked and disliked, and how she felt about her life. will.i.am ended up as executive producer on the album as well as co-writing some of the songs.

When pop star Rihanna heard Photographs, a song will.i.am had written for the Black Eyed Peas, she fell in love with it. At first, will.i.am didn't want to give the song to Rihanna, but she felt the song meant so much to her that she just kept on asking him until he agreed. 'When something is important to me, I'll go to the ends of the earth for it,' she said. The song, which is about the break-up of a relationship, is said to be one of her favourite recordings.

Recently, will.i.am collaborated with the stars of *Sesame Street* on a song called *What I Am*. Working with Elmo, Big Bird, Oscar the Grouch, Bert and Ernie to name a few, the song was about promoting a positive self-image. With the help of his puppet friends, will.i.am was able to encourage kids to keep their heads high and always follow their dreams.

That's Cool!

As a producer, will.i.am has also worked with Justin Bieber, Justin Timberlake, Nicki Minaj and Usher.

'ANYTHING CAN [IN]SPIRE ME IN MUSIC... [IT'S] LIKE PEOPLE... IT'S NOISE...IT JUST COMES.'

Fashion Icon

A man of style and originality, will.i.am is always wanting to stand out from the crowd, and has developed distinctive style for himself. He is particularly well-known for his outlandish stage outfits, edgy jackets and cool glasses. His keen interest in the fashion world is one he continues to follow.

Early on in his career, will.i.am studied at the Fashion Institute of Design and Merchandising (FIDM) in Los Angeles.
'I learned how to think about who you are designing for and who you are not designing for. A lot of times designers think they are designing for themselves. And that's a bad idea,' he explained.

During 2011, will.i.am worked with fashion designer Masatomo Yamaji on the Japanese brand Rynshu. The collection, which featured tailored jackets, slit-sleeve capes and harem pants, was described as both sophisticated and edgy.

The Coca-Cola Company and will.i.am have recently joined forces to launch Ekocycle. This is a fashion company that manufactures items made with at least 25 per cent recycled material made from Coca-Cola bottles. Will.i.am was inspired to get involved after seeing the amount of rubbish that was left behind after a Black Eyed Peas concert. The Ekocycle cloth is made by shredding plastic bottles into flakes and then shredding the flakes into thread.

Il.i.am tends the nch of OCYCLE

'WE NEEDED TO LOOK AT CULTURE AND GET BEHIND SOMETHING THAT PEOPLE COULD BE A PART OF... SOMETHING THAT THEY WANTED AND DESIRED.'

That's Cool!

Will.i.am's favourite fashion designer is Vivien Westwood who is known for bringing 1970s punk fashion into the mainstream. Her outlandish designs perfectly compliment his individual style.

The Voice

An artist like will.i.am knows a good thing when he hears it, which is why he was selected as one of the four coaches in BBC talent show, The Voice.

In March 2012, The Voice aired for the first time and was an instant success. The show's unique format meant that the judges had to listen to the contestants without seeing them. Only when a judge decided he or she wanted that contestant on their team could they turn around their chairs to see who was singing.

The coaches in the first two series of The Voice were: will.i.am, Jessie J, Danny O'Donoghue and Tom Jones. In the third series, the line-up changed, with Kylie Minogue and Ricky Wilson replacing Jessie and Danny.

Will.i.am proved to be a dedicated coach; he carefully nurtured and advised his team members and has remained in touch with his team finalists from the first two series, Tyler James and Leah McFall (neither of whom won).

Leah McFall, who was runner-up in series two of The Voice, has been working with will.i.am since appearing on the show. On 14 July 2013, she made her debut performance at the Wireless Festival in London's Hyde Park, alongside will.i.am. She also appeared as part of his #willpower tour in the European venues.

Will.i.am was visibly moved when his prodigy Jermain Jackman won The Voice in April 2014. He vowed to stick around to help him throughout his career. An emotional will.i.am said that he felt as if his grandma had put the two of them together from her place up in heaven.

When will.i.am took on the role of coach, he asked his friend Cheryl Cole, who was an X Factor judge, for advice:

'**I reached out to Cheryl for advice on keeping your cool, having a poker face, the importance of sticking with the singers – it's their dream. A lot of the times when you have other performers as part of the show, celebrities tend to want the shine, so they hog up time. So my whole thing was that I want to do *The Voice*, but I don't want to hog up time.**'

will.i.am
the Actor

A man of many talents, will.i.am has added actin to his list of achievements. Starting with appearances in Snickers advertisements alon with the Black Eyed Peas, it soon became clear that he was a natural.

IN 2008, WILL.I.AM PROVIDED THE VOICE FOR THE CHARACTER MOTO MOTO, THE SMOOTH-TALKING HIPPO IN DREAMWORKS ANIMATION'S MADAGASCAR: ESCAPE 2 AFRICA. WHEN ASKED HOW HE CAME UP WITH THE VOICE FOR THE CHARACTER. HE SAID:

'JUST GOOFING AROUND AND WHAT-NOT.'

HE ADDED THAT THE VOICE HE USED WAS SO UNLIKE HIS OWN THAT HIS NIECES PROBABLY WOULDN'T BELIEVE IT WAS ACTUALLY HIM. ALTHOUGH WILL.I.AM WAS VERY BUSY AT THE TIME, HE AGREED TO DO THE FILM BECAUSE HE IS A BIG FAN OF THE ANIMATED MOVIE MADAGASCAR.

'THIS IS SOMETHING I HAD TO MAKE TIME FOR,'

A NUMBER OF WILL.I.AM'S SONGS WERE USED IN THE MOVIE SOUNDTRACK INCLUDING THE TRAVELLING SONG, I LIKE TO MOVE IT, BIG & CHUNKY AND SHE LOVES ME.

2008

IN 2009, 20TH CENTURY FOX CAST WILL.I.AM IN HIS FIRST MOVIE ROLE. HE PLAYED THE PART OF JOHN WRAITH, OTHERWISE KNOWN AS KESTREL, IN X-MEN ORIGINALS: WOLVERINE. HIS FELLOW CAST MEMBERS WERE HUGH JACKMAN (WOLVERINE), LIEV SCHRIEBER (SABRETOOTH), DANNY HUSTON (WILLIAM STRYKER), RYAN REYNOLDS (DEADPOOL), TAYLOR KITSCH (GAMBIT) AND LYNN COLLINS (SILVER FOX).

'THE WHOLE CAST WAS AWESOME AND FOR THIS TO BE MY FIRST FOOT IN THE DOOR IN THE WORLD OF ACTING AND MOVIES, YOU KNOW, THIS IS BIG!'

2009

20 11

IN 2011, WILL.I.AM VOICED THE CHARACTER OF PEDRO, A RAPPING RED-CRESTED CARDINAL, FOR THE ANIMATION FILM *RIO*, WHICH WAS PRODUCED BY BLUE SKY STUDIOS. HIS SONG, *HOT WINGS (I WANNA PARTY)*, FEATURED IN THE SOUNDTRACK.WILL ALSO HAD A CAMEO ROLE IN THE ROMANTIC COMEDY *DATE NIGHT*, RELEASED IN 2010, IN WHICH HE APPEARED AS HIMSELF. THE FILM STARRED TINA FEY AND STEVE CARELL.

#DSA

That's Cool!

The character Kestrel is a mutant who has the power to teleport. Will.i.am said that if he could teleport in real life he'd go clubbing in different locations around the world always arriving at midnight – he'd stay for an hour and then find the next location where it was about to be midnight again.

Giving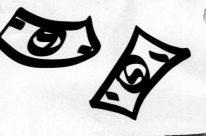
something back

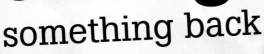

Though he is famous, will.i.am has not let it go to his head. He has always remembered where he came from and uses his celebrity status to help society wherever he can.

Philanthropy is high up on will.i.am's list of priorities. His i.am.angel foundation has joined forces with two American organizations – 'The California Endowment' and 'College Track' – to help 'TRANS4M' the youth community of Boyle Heights (the neighbourhood where will.i.am grew up).

The charity 'i.am.angel' also selects individuals to receive the 'i.am scholarship' – a program which has given over $500,000 in aid to college students. During the financial crisis in 2008, also known as the credit crunch, when many Americans lost their homes, the foundation launched the 'i.am home programme', which offers grants to struggling families and teaches people how to look after their money wisely.

That's Cool!

When asked if he might go into politics himself one day, will.i.am replied:

'Nope. I like it from this angle.'

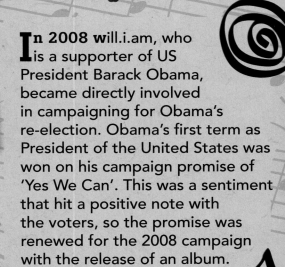

In 2008 will.i.am, who is a supporter of US President Barack Obama, became directly involved in campaigning for Obama's re-election. Obama's first term as President of the United States was won on his campaign promise of 'Yes We Can'. This was a sentiment that hit a positive note with the voters, so the promise was renewed for the 2008 campaign with the release of an album.

In 2013, will.i.am and 'College Track' launched an after-school club in Boyle Heights for the students of Roosevelt High School. 'College Track' is a national programme that allows students from poorer communities to reach their dream of obtaining a college degree. The new i.am College Track Boyle Heights Center supports over one hundred high school students during their time at college.

The album was called *Change is Now: Renewing America's Promise*. Will.i.am's contribution was a track called *It's a New Day* which was written as a tribute to Obama's initial victory. He performed it for the first time on *The Oprah Winfrey Show*. The lyrics of the song were written using words from Obama's speeches. Three million people watched the video on YouTube in the first week of its release!

Family
and Personal Life

Will.i.am was raised by his mother, Debra Cain, and his uncle Donny, and never met his father, William Adams. As well as two brothers and a sister, will.i.am has two adopted sisters and two adopted brothers. Debra gives credit to the people in their neighbourhood for helping to keep an eye on her young son. 'Boyle Heights was an ideal community at the time because he was sheltered by a lot of the neighbours who made sure he didn't get into different things,' she once explained.

When will.i.am became interested in music at the age of eight, his mother encouraged him to follow his dreams. She has described her relationship with him as one that goes way beyond mother and son. 'It's like we're best friends,' she said. Without his mother's strength behind him, will.i.am doesn't think he would have been able to accomplish all that he has.

'We feared our moms more than we did the police,' will.i.am once said. 'The police come round – whatever. But, my mom? That's it. You fear your mom. But not in a monster way, more in a not wanting to let them down kind of way.'

Will.i.am took his mother with him to President Obama's second presidential inauguration. The tweets he sent from that event demonstrate how proud he was to be able to do so:

'MY MOM NEVER THOUGHT WHEN WE WERE GROWING UP IN BOYLE HEIGHTS THAT WE WOULD GO TO THE WHITE HOUSE AND GO WITH THE PRESIDENT TO THE INAUGURATION, SO TO SHOW THAT TO MY MOM WAS AMAZING.'

'Took my mama to the White House and every step I took I wanted to cry… I'm so proud of our past. My mom did a good job… I could have been doing something totally different… but she raised me right… thanks mama.'

Will.i.am has also said:

'There's a family of influences that dictate behaviour. In the ghetto, there's a liquor store, a cheque-cashing place and a motel. What that tells you psychologically is, get a cheque, cash it, take a couple of steps, buy some liquor and get drunk, go home and get kicked out of your house. If you live in a good neighbourhood, you drive home and there's a bank, there's grocery stores and big houses – but no motels. What that tells you psychologically is, you protect your money and buy good things for your family to eat in your nice big house. So it's a different system.'

As soon as he could afford it, will.i.am moved his entire family to a nicer area of Los Angeles. This is something he had wanted to do since he was 12 years old.

Awards

A popular figure both with his many fans and within the music industry, will.i.am has been honoured with numerous awards for his work.

DAYTIME EMMY AWARDS

★ 2008, New Approaches in Daytime Entertainment: *Yes We Can*

★ 2011, Best Original Song: *What I Am*

GRAMMY AWARDS

★ 2005, Best Rap Performance by a Duo of Group: *Let's Get It Started,* the Black Eyed Peas

★ 2006, Best Rap Performance by a Duo of Group: *Don't Phunk with My Heart,* the Black Eyed Peas

★ 2007, Best Pop Performance by a Duo or Group with Vocals: *My Humps,* the Black Eyed Peas

★ 2009, Best Urban/Alternative Performance: *Be OK*

★ 2010, Best Short Form Music Video: *Boom Boom Pow,* the Black Eyed Peas

★ 2010, Best Pop Vocal Album: *The E.N.D,* the Black Eyed Peas

★ 2010, Best Pop Performance by a Duo of Group: *I Gotta Feeling,* the Black Eyed Peas

Will.i.am, Joss Stone, apl.de.ap and Recording Academy President Neil Portnow during the 47th Annual GRAMMY Awards nominations at the Music Box, LA, 7 December 2004

BMI AWARD

★ 2010, presented with the BMI President's Award in recognition of his work as an artist, producer and humanitarian. The honour is bestowed on individuals who have distinctly and profoundly influenced the entertainment industry.

KIDS CHOICE AWARDS

★ 2011, Favourite Band: The Black Eyed Peas

will.i.am

By now you should know lots of things about will.i.am. Test your knowledge of him by answering these questions:

1 In which are of Los Angeles did will.i.am grow up?

    a) Top Heights
    b) Boyle Heights
    c) Hollywood

2 What was the name of will.i.am's first group?

    a) Boyle Heights Buzz
    b) Blue Eyed Peas
    c) Atban Klan

3 What is the title of the Black Eyed Peas' first big hit?

    a) There's no Love
    b) Give me Love
    c) Where is the Love?

4 will.i.am was the first recording star to send a song to which planet?

    a) Mars
    b) Jupiter
    c) Saturn

5 What is will.i.am's mother's name?
    a) Susan
    b) Linda
    c) Debra

6 Which famous singer nagged will.i.am until he agreed to let her use the song *Photographs*?
    a) Rihanna
    b) Britney
    c) Beyoncé

7 On which TV talent show does will.i.am appear as a judge?
   a) Britain's Got Talent
   b) X Factor
   c) The Voice

8 When will.i.am was a kid he played American football for which team?
   a) LA Panthers
   b) East LA Bobcats
   c) Boyle Heights

9 Which superhero movie did will.i.am appear in?
   a) X-Men Originals: Wolverine
   b) The Amazing Spiderman
   c) Iron Man

10 In which year was will.i.am born?
   a) 1975
   b) 1979
   c) 1982

Answers

1   b) Boyle Heights
2   c) Atbam Klann
3   c) *Where is the Love?*
4   a) Mars
5   c) Debra
6   a) Rihanna
7   c) *The Voice*
8   b) East LA Bobcats
9   a) *X-Men Originals: Wolverine*
10   a) 1975

Read about will.i.am in the following books:

will.i.am: The Unauthorized Biography by Danny White (Michael O'Mara Books Limited, 2012)

Let's Get It Started: The Rise and Rise of the Black Eyed Peas by Daryl Easlea (Omnibus Press, 2012)

You can find out more information about will.i.am by:
Logging onto http://will.i.am/ and http://iamangelfoundation.org/ or following him on Twitter @iamwill

Quote sources

Page 4 the Jonathan Ross Show, 2013; **Page 7** EG Entertainment, YouTube, 2011, The Jonathan Ross Show, 2013, Boyle Heights Beat, 2013; **Page 8** The Jonathan Ross Show, 2013; **Page 9** The Jonathan Ross Show, 2013; **Page 14** Access Hollywood, 2006, contactmusic.com, 2009; **Page 15** E! Pop Innovators, YouTube; **Page 17** Billboard.com 2012; **Page 19** Graham Norton Show, 2012; **Page 20** Dreamworks publicity interview, 2008, MTV News, 2008; **Page 22** Time Magazine, 2009; **Page 24** Contactmusic.com, 2010; **Page 25** Hello Magazine, 2013, The Jonathan Ross Show, 2013

Glossary

BMI (Broadcast Music, Inc.)
An American organization that collects royalties (payments) for artists

Bobcat
A North American wild cat

Boyle Heights
An area of government housing in East Los Angeles

Collaborate
To work with someone else on a project

Credit crunch
A name invented to describe the economic downturn of 2008

Debut
A first performance in public

Elementary school
Infant school

Emmy award
A television industry award in the USA

Grammy award
A music industry award in the USA

High school
Secondary school from age 14

Hispanic
Spanish-speaking or of Spanish origin

Kindergarten
Nursery school

Middle school
A school between elementary and high school in the USA for ages 11 to 14

NASA
National Aeronautics and Space Administration – the American space agency

Outlandish
Unfamiliar, strange or bizarre

Philanthropist
A person who donates generously of their time and money to promote the well-being of others

Red-crested cardinal
A South American bird with a bright red chest and head

Scholarship
Financial help with fees for education

Tacos
Traditional Mexican food of a corn or wheat tortilla folded around a filling

INDEX